When's this place gonna get Smooth?

29 Parenting Lessons We Learned the Hard Way...

Rodney Kennedy
B.A., Louisiana College
Ph.D., Louisiana State University
Education Consultant

Johnelle Kennedy
B.S., Louisiana State University
M.S., Southeastern Louisiana University
Principal, Westdale Elementary
Baton Rouge, Louisiana

This book is dedicated to
our children

Vin, Kirkland, Melissa, Jennifer and Jeffrey

The Up With Youth Company
1975 W. Muriel Street
Baton Rouge, LA 70816
800-538-7107
For more information on
Parenting Workshops, call 1-800-538-7107

ISBN 1-886901-06-6

Cover design by Ellen Murphy Bennett

Introduction

"When's this place gonna get smooth?" A house we moved into was in need of repairs. The ceiling above Kirkland's bed looked like it would fall on his head. As Johnelle helped him with his prayers, as she did every night, three year old Kirkland asked, **"When's this place gonna get smooth?"** We ask that about parenting all the time. Parenting may be the hardest job in the world. After 30 something years in the parenting journey, we are convinced that most lessons are learned the hard way. Children enter the world, as gifts to parents, but they do not come with care and maintenance instructions. Imagine the incongruence of a society that provides 120 page manuals for maintaining mini-vans, but not a word for caring about a new baby. The day mom and baby leave the hospital, what do you get? Three Pampers®, a used baby bottle, a $25 free gift package (that was actually on the itemized statement), and a $7,000 bill.

When the second child comes along, there is the temptation to believe that parenting will now be easier since there is experience on our side. Wrong. Each child is so unique, so different.

Armed with the knowledge that our children are strong-willed, uninterested in pleasing us, and determined to get their own way, we work on maintaining a patient, low-key, calm approach. Our lifelong guidelines for parenting: Be trustworthy, be truthful, no put downs of any kind, a few rules and consequences, and lots and lots of affection.

As the keepers of the home, parents have the responsibility to:

- **Keep it simple**
- **Keep it straight**
- **Keep your word**
- **Keep it smooth whenever possible**

Remember parenting is hard work. Time, energy, effort and stubbornness are required. And a measure of grace and hope. May the parenting journey reward you with some smooth places.

We're not going to...
1. Scream and yell

A movie advertisement caught my eye: **"SCREAMERS".**

"Look, a movie about parenting." Actually the movie was science fiction. Doesn't parenting sometimes feel like science fiction or a horror story? Children have a way of stepping on our last nerve.

Before we realize what's happening, the decibel level in the home registers on the seismograph at the local university. All that yelling and screaming creates chaos. Even more destructive is the loss of respect - parents and children.

The good thoughts are spoken softly:

- **I love you.**
- **You're beautiful.**
- **Next time it will be better.**
- **I'm sorry.**
- **Can we start over?**
- **I appreciate you.**
- **Thank you.**
- **You're welcome.**

Our family lives by the **NSR** - the "No Screaming Rule". If all attempts to stop yelling and screaming fail, we'll send you the SCREAMATROL PATCH. Put it under your arm and in twenty-one days you'll reach the point where you will be able to stop screaming.

Good luck!

We're not going to...
2. Lecture our children

Lectures produce the glazed look of bored audiences. Their bodies are still in the building, but their minds have taken a trip. Next time you catch yourself wagging a finger in the face of a child, realize you are about to give a lecture. Take advantage of the warning signal and give yourself a break. No lectures. At least make that one of your parenting goals.

Refraining from lecturing can be hard because the self-gratification is so high. And sometimes children seem to be begging for a good lecture. If you have to give a lecture, remember the kids are not listening.

Recently I slipped into the lecture mode: "Son, I don't know how to tell you how disappointed I am, but sit down because I'm about to try."

Mostly, though, remember, that the mini-lecture, at best, is only a slight stress reducer for the parent.

We're not going to...
3. Berate our children's best effort

Given the pressure to succeed, to be number one, to compete at the highest levels, I am not surprised at the high levels of stress in children today. Johnelle, attending a Little League Baseball game, overheard an agitated Mom scream, "You better hit that ball or you won't get any supper tonight."

Competitive rituals are the natural result of the religious fervor engendered by love of sports.
Is there not something amiss when a U. S. A. athlete wins a silver medal at the Olympics only to be criticized for not winning the gold? Somehow being second best in the entire world is unacceptable.

Perhaps our children are our best teachers. Kirkland, after much "parental support", turned in a project for International Day to his third grade teacher. Ireland was his country of choice. He dressed as a leprechaun and everything. When Johnelle picked him up from school, she discovered that he had made a "B" on the project. With as much positive tact as possible, she asked, "Kirkland, what do you think Mr. Genco wanted to do for an "A" on your project?" Kirkland looked at Johnelle as if she were the world's least intelligent Mom, and said, "Mama! Who cares? B's are great!!!"

Give the kids a break. Competition is not the chief virtue in life. Being number one is not the only valid reason for living. Children have worth and value simply because they are. As Lewis Thomas suggests: a human child, one human child anywhere in the world, is the greatest modern wonder of the universe.

Enjoy sports with your children. But teach them cooperation.

We're not going to...
4. Bribe our children

To bribe a child is an act of desperation. Of course desperation is a constant companion of the parenting journey. Cookies to stop crying in the supermarket. Candy to put an end to temper tantrums. Dollars for grades. One Father, participating in a parenting workshop, insisted, "I got me a valedictorian paying for grades." Not bad results. He probably, however, could have accomplished the same goal in another, more positive way, and saved a lot of money.

Buying grades or buying good behavior sounds like begging - a way of negotiating from weakness.
"I'm not in charge. Please behave. Please don't make a fool out of me in public."
"I'll give you whatever you want if you'll just shut up."

A two year old recognizes and grasps power handed to her by a defeated parent. Kids will pull your string as long as you let them. A Mom told me that a two year old was in charge at her house. She forgot a basic principle: Never negotiate with terrorists or toddlers. One will bomb you; the other will drive you insane.

Lewis Thomas, in **Late Night Thoughts While Listening to Mahler's Ninth**, suggests that altruism is in the human genes. Well, I hope he is right. Why? Because when parents bribe children for goodness sake, they teach them that goodness is always rewarded with material benefits. Children become adults expecting to be paid for goodness and lacking compassion and mercy.
"You better be good 'cause Santa Claus is coming to town."

If altruism is in the genes, we have something to build on. Children can learn to do good because it is good to do good, because we are created for goodness.

We're not going to...
5. Forget to show plenty of affection

Primary parenting task: to bless our children. That blessing, from the religious perspective, is an act of laying on of hands. Aha! The power of touch. There is no substitute for the touch of love. The warmth, the comfort, the sense of security combine to give a child a sense of belonging in the world.

I know grown people who would be emotionally well if their fathers' would hold them and rock them and say, "I love you." Hugs can take the bugs out of plenty of faulty parenting models. Spread affection everywhere. Dad can do a lot for his children by showing them how much he loves Mom.

Even St. Paul, as grizzled as he often was, exhorted Christians, *"Greet one another with a holy kiss."* Hugs and kisses are acts of holiness and wholeness.

Need examples of spreading affection?

- **Read to your children. Every day.**
- **Listen carefully.**
- **Take them special places for no particular reason.**
- **Spend time doing stuff the kids love to do. Get beat at video games.**
- **Affirm their worthiness.**
- **Update your own sense of wonder.**

After all, affection, with her attendants, hugs, smiles, and lots of humor, is the critical life support principle.

We're not going to...
6. Argue with our children

"Never argue with children" is our basic rule.

As an elementary school principal and a Mom I have learned that arguing with children is a sure loser. Rod, on the other hand, has been a slow learner. Trained as a debater, he thrills at the opportunity to argue with anyone, anytime, anywhere. Sensing the kill, he will go straight for the exposed weakness.

Did you know that our common human language about arguing is built around an ordinary metaphor: Argument is war? I challenge you to talk about argument without using the language of war: attack, defend, defeat, belittle, tear apart.

Besides argument easily degenerates to verbal abuse, sarcasm, and meanness. The family loses when parents argue with children. Ever cleaned up after a war? Arguing with children is not a fair fight. The kids win.

You are an adult. You are reasonable. You are logical. You are mature. They are not interested in the subtleties of logic and reason. Children argue irrationally. They pull adults into that mud hole of emotionalism. Before we know what's happening we are reduced to emotional basket cases.

Never argue with children.

We're not going to...
7. Be timid about our beliefs

The Second Testament of the Bible has a pair of letters named Timothy. St. Paul, writing to encourage timid Timothy, says, **"For God has not given us a spirit of timidity, but of power and love and discipline."**

We decided that since our children's minds are going to be filled with something, they definitely would get a complete exposure to our beliefs. We were not interested in teaching our children what to believe, but the importance of believing. We are tolerant, accepting people; but we do have strong beliefs. Our children have received large dosages of Christianity - the United Methodist version - along with a full menu of social activism and compassion, especially for the poor and the oppressed. They were taught that politics is a good word and that liberal is an even better word. Even more, our children have been exposed to our philosophy of the common good. We are here to serve the common good.

Maintain a passion for the conversation about beliefs. Don't back down. Affirm your faith. Gigantic affirmations always are needed in an age of cynicism.

We're not going to...
8. Lighten up on the teaching

Bombarded with a multiplicity of confusing truth claims, values, opinions, and assumptions, children need the steady, consistent teaching of their parents.

As our children's primary teachers, we want to give them the tools they need to think creatively. Lifeskills, good manners, civility, compassion, understanding - all these and more we want to pass on to our children. We want them to think for themselves and learn to solve problems without blaming other people.

Two fourth graders were explaining the reasons they got into a fight at school. As usual there were two different stories about the one fight. Then one youngster interrupted to say, "It's not my fault. He made me hit him." Blaming others robs children of the opportunity to be responsible human beings. So teach, teach, and teach your children.

Don't expect a lot of gratitude or understanding. A principal in St. Mary's, Pennsylvania told us about a first grader who got up from his chair at noon on the first day of school, put on his coat, and headed for the door. The teacher stopped him and asked him where he was going. "I going home," came the reply. As a kindergarten student he only went to school for half a day each day. So now he was ready to go home.

The teacher carefully went over the fact that first grade students stayed all day. "We're going to lunch and then spend the rest of the afternoon in class." Convinced, but still puzzled, the young student asked, "I just want to know, who signed me up for this?"

We're not going to...
9. Tolerate a messy house

Go ahead and call us obsessive-compulsive or any other psychobabble term you may have picked up from reading **Psychology Today**. From where we sit, in the den of a lovely home, a messy house gets a family out of the daily routines that give life and purpose. That doesn't imply that your house has to pass the white glove test and be so clean people are afraid to sit on the furniture or use oxygen in your formal living room.

Spend a few minutes each morning or evening putting things back where they belong. A few simple rules will suffice:

- **Keep the pathways through the house uncluttered.**
- **No dirty dishes in the sink or on the counter.**
- **Nothing left on the breakfast room table.**
- **Clean up your own mess.**
- **Keep the bathroom clean, especially the lid.**
- **Pay the maid well and keep her in cleaning supplies.**

We're not going to...
10. Talk the language of our teenagers

A country radio station disc jockey, interviewing a car salesman (I have a lot to do early in the morning - drive time, O. K.?), said the word "Cool" at least 9 times. Each time the high-pitched screech sounded like "Kuuol" or a bad cough.

Every generation is entitled to their own particular jargon. If they are lucky enough they will create new words that gain official acceptance in the English dictionary. We simply refuse to talk like our children.

But we will use one piece of advice our kids spout regularly: **Don't go there.**

We're not going to...
11. Leave an unmade bed

Of all the times Mom was right, the bed making rule is the really big one. For some reason I hate making the bed. Some days, when Johnelle left for work before I got out of bed, I would sneak out, and leave the bed unmade. Then I'd make sure I was home early enough to make the bed before she came home.

As a single guy I bought a king size bed. That way I could sleep on one side for a week and then sleep on the other side for a week without having to change the sheets.

I'm better now. With so much chaos in the world, I try to give some order to our corner of the world. So now I make the bed. And I always have clean underwear.

We're not going to...

12. Pretend we have it all together

We do not believe in having it all together. Life is unfinished, unrehearsed business all the way.

People who think they have it all together are under a lot of stress trying to hold it all together. They believe they are the true ancestors of the Puritans. Their rigid moralism makes them gimlet-eyed critics who believe God put them on earth to see to it that everyone who's got it coming gets it. Stay away from such people.

We prefer some surprises. Let the good times roll. Trés bien.

We're not going to...
13. Spend our lives at the office

The office is a safer place because there are no children to parent and to discipline and to raise. The office is easier than parenting.

Still there is too much life beyond the office to allow ourselves to get stuck there. Whatever we leave at the office will be patiently waiting for us when we return.

Go there. Work there. Do your best at the office. Do not live there.

Your children are waiting at home. Go there often. Stay there as much as possible.

We're not going to...
14. Give up telling stories

Stories are wonderful. Especially those you can tell over and over again.
While we resist telling autobiographical tales during discipline moments,
we refuse to stop telling stories to our children. We have a tradition to pass along.

Our grown children can pick and choose among family traditions. For the time being, that being the time while we are still alive, there are some stories and traditions that will remain alive and active. Every Christmas we will watch the story, "It's A Wonderful Life." We will tell our children stories about their grandparents. And we will tell them our own personal stories, selected from our own highly edited versions.

God loves stories. That must be why he invented us. Tell the old stories.
Your kids need the connection.

We're not going to...

15. Teach our children bigotry, prejudice, or racism

Bigots live in their own little world. Such people draw ever smaller circle to exclude different folks.

For us there is only one family - the human one. We all fell out of the same tree. Adam (Everyman) is our father and Eve (Everywoman) is our mother.
"God made of one blood all nations of the earth."

Draw the circles huge. Somewhere Emerson put it,
"Not until the sun excludes you do I exclude you."
Works for us.

We're not going to...

16. Take our children to restaurants before they are ready

Children and nice restaurants do not make good partners. Small children, especially, are **Not Ready for Restaurant Time**. McDonald's provides a service for parents with small children - a play area (indoors no less) and a happy meal.

For us a happy meal is a quiet French restaurant in a lovely white board cottage, a class of white wine, soft music, stimulating conversation, and fine food. At least once a week go out to dinner - adults only.

As long as children are intent on embarrassing you in public, pay the extra bucks for the baby-sitter. Take Mom to the restaurant and leave the kids at home.

Frequent restaurants with this sign:

- **No pets**
- **No children**
- **No smoking**

We're not going to...

17. Cheat our children out of the privilege of doing chores

Why did you have children? We had children to get help!!! Both of us have demanding careers. Someone has to do the chores. What could be more important in a child's development? As soon as a kid is old enough to walk, follow simple instructions, and strong enough to carry a load, give him/her a chore.

Chores are the contributions each member of the family makes to the team effort. We do not pay our children to do the chores. That sends the wrong message.

Helping out at home is another version of homework. It is expected and deserves praise when completed. "Thank you!" "Good job!" Never rob your children of the privilege of working hard. There is no free ride.

If you worry that children won't like doing chores, put your mind at ease. Of course they won't like working. Might as well learn early. If we only did what we liked, not much would get done.

When our children graduate from college, we are sure they will want to put a footnote on their resume: **Trust me I know how to work hard**. I've heard that corporations pay good money for people with a strong work ethic.

We're not going to...

18. Wallow in guilt over our children's mistakes and failures

The journey that moves children from dependence to independence can be litter with bad judgments, bad calls, and big failures. **There are lessons we all learn the hard way.**

Do your best raising children, but please know that these strong, assertive, stubborn children are going to make mistakes. When that happens allow them to face the music and give them second chances. But do not wallow in guilt over the mistakes of your children.

Grieve for the pain of your children. Help bear their heavy loads, but do not take on guilt as a managing partner.

The next time you are sitting in the bed at 2:30 in the morning, eating a pint of vanilla ice cream from the container, crying, "I'm ruining my children," stop it. Eat the ice cream but stop your whining. The added pounds are preferable to the unnecessary guilt. Cut yourself some slack. You are a better parent than you give yourself credit for being.

After all you are reading our book. Thanks!

We're not going to...
19. Lose our cool

An out-of-control parent can not help an out-of-control child.

Take deep breaths. Calm yourself. Don't discipline when you are angry. When we are mad we make bad decisions.

Postpone the discipline until you are in control of yourself. In Southern slang, "Don't let kids get your goat."

The time you use to calm down before speaking to your children will be good discipline. We call it "letting them sweat." Children waiting for discipline become very quiet and apprehensive. What they imagine is far worse than the discipline actually ever is.

We're not going to...

20. Hover over our children like helicopters

Parenting stress often comes from micromanagement. Chill! Give your children some breathing space. They are bright, creative, intelligent. Allow them to discover life.

Protect without becoming overprotective. Encourage but do not hover. Guide and nurture, but let children solve problems for themselves. Life can be a puzzle. Solve it without looking at the answers in advance.

Remember the answers keep changing for each new generation.

We're not going to...
21. Allow our children to be in charge

Prior to arrival, children are packaged with POWER software. No sooner do they come home from the hospital, than they struggle to take charge. One of our strong-willed children, in our faded memory, was born complaining about the temperature in the delivery room and has been in a bad mood ever since.

Prepare for the invasion of the kid tricks. In our parenting research (observing parents abusing their children at Wal-Mart), we have witnessed lots of kid tricks.

The child cries and the parent gives the child a bag of chocolate chip cookies.
We call this trick **and** treat.

Keep a list of the tricks your children pull. If they fool you once, accept defeat graciously. If they fool you twice or more, give us a call. A parenting seminar is coming your way soon. Be there!

We're not going to...

22. Forget the basic rule: Enjoy your children

Sam Keen believes the "gift of delight" is basic emotional food for children. We agree. Children are meant to be enjoyed even as we endure the trials of parenting. Our primary parenting task is to enjoy our children.

What then is the "gift of delight"? Borrowing again from Keen and Barbara Colorosa, we define "gift of delight" in seven daily delight statements.

- **You are welcome in our space** ***(Does not include our king size bed.)***
- **You matter a great deal to us.**
- **You are adored and loved.**
- **You are listened to, really listened to.**
- **We believe in you.**
- **We trust you.**
- **We know you can handle life's challenges.**

And the overriding delight principle:

- **LIFE AS IT IS GIVEN IS GOOD.**

We realize children can set your mind into a negative spin, just like a tilt-a-whirl. Those tough times when you want to scream and yell, dispense large dosages of delight.

Keep repeating to yourself:
"My children are gifts from God. Gifts from God. Gifts from God. I love my children. I love my children. I do. I do. I do."

We're not going to...
23. Interrupt when one of the children is pouting

Of all the tricks children pull our favorite is pouting. Why? Because it is so quiet. A pouting child goes to her room and leaves us with a quiet, peaceful evening of quality time. Enjoy.

The next time your child pouts, find your spouse, walk together to the den, turn down the lights, throw the remote control under the sofa, and spend time developing intimacy. Your child will peek out her bedroom door to see if you're coming. Wave at her, asking, "How's the pouting going?"

Surprise your children. Let'em pout. They will recover. In fact, children have selective, short-term memory about defeat. At breakfast the next morning the pout will be replaced with a smile.

Don't be puzzled. Enjoy the moment. You deserve it.

We're not going to...

24. Fall victim to the illusion that we are on this earth to fulfill our children's material fantasies

Children ask for everything under the sun. "Dad, will you go to the Dodge store and buy me a 1997 Dodge Ram pickup with a V-8, roll bars, and running boards?" That request, from a normal sixteen-year-old son, was handled with ease. I did not even need to ask his mother for parental support. "Read my lips. NO."

Children are allergic to NO! But with practice they get better. There are times when they need to learn the joy of expectation, the power of delayed gratification. Say NO when necessary. When your children walk through the den, in front of the television you are trying to watch, smile, look up at them, and say, "NO!"

"What, Dad?"

"Nothing in particular. I'm just practicing."

We were not put on the planet to give our children all their material fantasies, and we don't have to leave them a fortune. The can earn their own. We are spending ours.

What—Did you think we should save for a big funeral?

We're not going to...

25. Be autobiographical during discipline moments

My dad, Johnelle's favorite father-in-law, claims he walked barefoot to school every day - a sixteen mile round trip. Among his more dubious autobiographical tales - "I walked barefoot to school in the snow every winter." Considering the fact that Louisiana does not manage one decent snowfall per year, that is real distorted memory.

Children do not connect with autobio stories during discipline.

Our time differs from children time. As Gibran puts it:

Your children are not your children.
They are the sons and daughters of Life's longing for itself.
They come through you but not from you,
and though they are with you, yet they belong not to you.
You must give them your love but not your thoughts,
for they have their own thoughts . . .
you may strive to be like them, but seek not to make them like you.
For life goes not backward nor tarries with yesterday.

We're not going to...
26. Dispense illusions

Our sewer systems would never recover if they were required to sift through and dispense with the daily truck loads of illusions passed along. Children deserve better than the party line.

If we start early enough, like when the baby is still in the womb (reading exercises), telling the truth to our children, they will become experts in recognizing con jobs from their peers and other adults. Armed with truth and critical thinking skills, our children will not buy into every illusion peddled by advertisers, politicians, or other assorted medicine men.

We will have to work hard to overcome our own attraction to illusion. After all we are the purveyors of the illusion of affluence - that haunting concept that money produces happiness. No wonder people buy things they do not need, with money they do not have, to impress people they do not like.

In the straightforward words of Marian Wright Edelman,

"Be honest.
Struggle to live what you say and preach.
Call things by their right names.
Be moral examples for your children."

The older we get, the more likely we are to say to people, "Cut the bull."

We're not going to...

27. Let our children stay home from church

An obscure sense of rebellion against the church because we were made to go as children is no reason to cheat our own kids of the particular agony-ecstasy of worship. Besides childhood memories are neither mature or reliable - not even under hypnosis.

Take children by the hand and take them to church or synagogue. "This is a family thing. We worship together." Give a child lots of the singing, praying, communing, and preaching of the church, no matter how abominable that sometimes sounds. If your pastor's sermons are that bad, send him/her some good stories.

Children can go or not go to church after they have enough personal evidence to make a responsible decision. If they go away during college and early adult life, do not be surprised to seem them back in the pew later. That is more likely, of course, if they attended church as children.

Besides church is only one hour once a week. O. K., two if you go to Church School. As Mark Twain suggested we can stand anything for an hour.

We're not going to...

28. Hide our feelings or discount our children's feelings

In some families feelings are, at best, belittled; at worst, they are discounted. Children submerge feelings onto the subconscious nether world where those feelings incubate and later come forth in more vicious, horrible manifestations.

We sometimes say to each other, "Don't tell me how to feel." That is actually good advice. A person's feelings are legitimate. There is nothing wrong with feeling. Actually, you can no more stop a feeling than you can stop a thought from entering your mind.

Help children express and verbalize their feelings. When you are angry, say so without yelling and screaming but in an angry tone of voice. When you are upset or disappointed, communicate your feelings. Children learn from parents whether the expression of feelings is permitted.

For generations little boys in the South were taught, "Big boys don't cry." In other words, "Keep your feelings to yourself." Help your sons know that crying is O. K. We say to our children, "We understand how you feel . . ."

We're not going to...
29. Lose the sense of wonder

May we ever maintain the sense of wonder.

Watch hummingbirds fly backward. How do they do that? Watch spiders weave webs. Make a list of the seven modern wonders of the world.

Stay young. Pay kids' games. Lose at the games kids play.

Laugh. A lot. When the laughter dies, so does the wonder.

Learn. As much as possible.

Love. There always a need for more.

May the dazzling grace that always is shine in your hearts.

Blessings!